GETTING TO KNOW
THE WORLD'S
GREATEST COMPOSERS

DUKE
ELLINGTON

WRITTEN AND ILLUSTRATED BY MIKE VENEZIA

CONSULTANT

DONALD FREUND, PROFESSOR OF COMPOSITION, INDIANA UNIVERSITY SCHOOL OF MUSIC

CHILDRENS PRESS®
CHICAGO

Picture Acknowledgments

Music on the cover, Stock Montage, Inc.; 3, The Bettmann Archive;
5, Victor Haboush; 11, AP/Wide World Photos; 12, Art and Artifacts
Division, Schomburg Center for Research in Black Culture,
The New York Public Library, Astor, Lenox and Tilden Foundations;
13, National Museum of American Art, Smithsonian Institution,
Gift of the Harmon Foundation; 14-15, Frank Driggs Collection;
18, Culver Pictures, Inc.; 19, UPI/Bettmann; 21, Frank Driggs
Collection; 28, The Bettmann Archive; 31, © Duncan P. Schiedt;
32, AP/Wide World Photos

Project Editor: Shari Joffe
Design: PCI Design Group, San Antonio, Texas
Photo Research: Jan Izzo

Library of Congress Cataloging–in–Publication Data

Venezia, Mike.
    Duke Ellington / written and illustrated by Mike Venezia.
    p.   cm. -- (Getting to know the world's greatest composers)
    Summary: Traces the life of the internationally acclaimed musician
    and composer who helped popularize jazz music.
    ISBN 0-516-04540-7 (lib. bdg.)—ISBN 0-516-44540-5 (pbk.)
    1. Ellington, Duke, 1899-1974--Juvenile literature.
    2. Jazz musicians--United States--Biography--Juvenile literature.
    [1. Ellington, Duke, 1899-1974. 2. Musicians. 3. Composers.
    4. Afro-Americans--Biography.] I. Title. II. Series: Venezia, Mike.
    Getting to know the world's greatest composers.
    ML3930.E44V46 1995
    781.65'092--dc20
    [B]   95-2404
                            CIP
                            AC MN

Duke Ellington in 1933

Edward Kennedy "Duke" Ellington was born in Washington, D.C., the capital of the United States, in 1899. He is known for his piano playing, bandleading, and especially for being one of America's greatest composers.

The type of music Duke Ellington became famous for is called *jazz*. Jazz is an original American style of music that started right around the time Duke was born. It was invented by African Americans in the city of New Orleans. Jazz started out by taking bits and pieces of many different musical styles. Often, jazz music has a loud brass-band sound that was inspired by marching bands in New Orleans. It usually has an exciting rhythm and powerful expressive feeling that comes from two styles of music: ragtime and blues.

The Jazz Expression,
by Victor Haboush

Most importantly, jazz has a sound
that comes right from each musician's
beliefs and experiences. People found
that jazz was great fun to listen to and
dance to, and it became very popular.

Edward Kennedy "Duke" Ellington grew up in a loving family. He was very close to his mother. She always encouraged him, and made sure he was brought up the right way. From his father, Duke learned a lot of manners, proper grammar, and a stylish way of talking. Mr. Ellington was an experienced butler who had even worked at the White House when Teddy Roosevelt was president.

While he was growing up, Duke was mostly interested in baseball and art. One day, after Duke was accidentally hit in the head with a baseball bat, Mrs. Ellington decided to start Duke on piano lessons. She thought it would be a much safer activity. Duke, however, didn't care for piano lessons at all as a kid, and his parents finally gave up on him.

It wasn't until he was a teenager that Duke became interested in the piano. One day he got a chance to hear a new hot piano player named Harvey Brooks. Harvey was about the same age as Duke, and impressed him so much that Duke decided to give the piano another chance, right away.

Duke learned to play the piano pretty much on his own. He got advice from talented local piano players, as well as from some who were passing through Washington, D.C., on their way to and from jobs.

Duke wrote and performed his first song for a high-school dance. It went over very well. Duke was proud that a song he had written was well liked, and he enjoyed being the center of attention. Even though Duke was interested in becoming an artist and was even offered a scholarship to an important art school, he decided to try and make music his career. He began writing as many new songs as he could.

It was right around this time that
Edward Kennedy Ellington got his
nickname. A friend told him that it
was important for popular music
composers to have a catchy name.
"Duke" seemed to fit Edward Kennedy
Ellington because of his stylish and
gentlemanly ways. Many famous jazz

musicians have had nicknames that describe something about them or their music, like Fats Waller, Jelly Roll Morton, Tricky Sam Nanton, Count Basie, Willie "the Lion" Smith, Louis "Satchmo" Armstrong, Dizzy Gillespie, and many more.

Around 1917, Duke and some of his friends formed a small band called the Washingtonians. They played at parties, dances, and clubs all over Washington, D.C. In 1918, Duke got married. He and his wife, Edna, had a son, Mercer, in 1919.

Jazz trumpeter Louis Armstrong (right), shown here with Duke, was nicknamed "Satchmo"—a shortened form of "satchel mouth"—because his smile was said to be as big as a large purse!

Jockey Club, a scene of Harlem nightlife
in 1929, by Archibald J. Motley, Jr.

Duke knew that in order to make
it as a musician, and be able to
support his family, he and his friends
would have to go to New York City.
New York was where all the great
jazz bands were playing.

Jitterbugs No. 2,
by William Johnson, 1939-40

Duke loved the excitement and glamour of New York, especially a section called Harlem.

Harlem was where African Americans could live without having to worry about being looked down on or treated badly, as they were in most other cities at this time. Many black doctors, lawyers, teachers, writers, artists, and musicians moved to Harlem. They created an exciting time in history that became known as the Harlem Renaissance.

When the Washingtonians first got to New York, it was almost impossible to get a job, because there were so many musicians around. Jazz players from New Orleans, Chicago, and St. Louis heard they could make more money in the dance halls and nightclubs of New York. The Washingtonians kept trying, though, and finally their luck changed. Duke and the Washingtonians were hired to play in a well-known nightspot called Barron's Exclusive Club. They did very well, and were soon offered jobs in other popular nightclubs.

The Washingtonians in New York City in 1925

Things were going great for Duke, and got even better when a new trumpet player joined the band. His name was James "Bubber" Miley. Before Bubber came into the band, the Washingtonians' music was fairly quiet and moody with some ragtime thrown in once in a while for people to dance to. It wasn't really jazz music, which is what all the nightclubs really wanted.

Not only did Bubber Miley know a lot about jazz, he also made a very special sound with his instrument. Bubber was able to make a growling noise and use

a mute to create a wild kind of
sound that few trumpet players
had done before or since. A mute
is a device attached to a musical
instrument to soften or muffle its
tone. In the 1920s, a mute was just
the end of a bathroom plunger that
was put over the end of a horn.

The entrance to Harlem's Cotton Club

Bubber Miley gave Duke's band a wild, hot jazz sound that was much different from other bands of the day. It's easy to hear Bubber's playing in such popular Duke Ellington recordings as "East St. Louis Toodle-oo" and "Black and Tan Fantasy."

By 1927, the Washingtonians had changed their name to the Duke Ellington Orchestra, and were playing at the Cotton Club—the most famous nightclub in New York! Duke began to bring other new members into the band, and was writing one hit song after another.

Duke Ellington (seated at piano) and his band

One thing that made Duke Ellington's band different from just about any other jazz band of the time was that Duke made sure to surround himself with the best musicians he could find—musicians like Bubber Miley, who could make a one-of-a-kind sound with their instruments.

Duke would listen to his members play different parts of the music he wrote until it sounded just right to him. Duke played his band kind of like an instrument, giving his players a chance to do their own special thing.

Duke with drummer
Sonny Greer in 1940

This not only gave Duke's music a unique jazz sound, but made his band members feel good about being an important part of each musical piece.

Another thing Duke did well was to mix the different instrumental sounds in his band. Many jazz experts have compared this to mixing colors—or painting with sound. When you close your eyes and listen to music, you can sometimes picture colors. A cool clarinet sound might remind you of the color blue. A hot sound from a trumpet might remind you of blazing red, and saxophone notes remind some people of liquid gold!

A good example of Duke mixing musical
sound-colors is a piece called "The Mooche."
Because Duke had once been interested
in being an artist, colors were always
important to him. Many of Duke's pieces,
including "Mood Indigo," "Black and Tan
Fantasy," and "Magenta Haze," have colors
in their titles.

Often, Duke and his musicians would have a picture in mind or would be telling a story when they composed or played their music. In one famous piece called "Harlem Airshaft," Duke expressed all the exciting daily activities he saw and heard going on in a Harlem apartment building. When you hear "Harlem Airshaft," it's fun to listen to the different instruments jumping around and changing moods. Duke did this to give his piece the feeling of energy and life in a busy apartment building.

By 1940, Duke Ellington had one of the most popular bands in the United States. They made radio broadcasts, records, and appearances all over the country. Unfortunately, in many of the cities where Duke played, there were people who were prejudiced against African Americans. Sometimes Duke and his band had a hard time getting hotel rooms or service in a restaurant. Duke refused to be treated badly and decided to travel with his band

members in their own private train cars. The railroad would leave Duke's cars parked on an unused track until they were ready to move on. Now Duke and his orchestra could eat, sleep, and live comfortably when they arrived in a strange and unfamiliar town.

As it turned out, Duke loved traveling by train. He got lots of ideas for new songs by listening to the train's sounds as it rolled along, and by looking out over the beautiful scenery as it passed by.

Duke Ellington's music was as popular as ever until the 1950s. Then people started becoming more interested in new types of music, like rock and roll. Duke's style of jazz seemed old-fashioned to many younger people, and some jazz experts thought Duke Ellington's best music was behind him.

Duke writing music

Duke was disappointed, but
never gave up. He worked as
hard as ever, writing music and
working with his band. Finally,
in 1956, something happened
that put Duke back on top again.

Duke was invited to play the closing music for a jazz festival in Newport, Rhode Island. It was late at night when Duke and his orchestra came on stage to play. People in the audience were tired and some of them were beginning to go home. Duke knew that in order to get people's attention, he would have to do something pretty special. Duke gave his saxophone player, Paul Gonsalves, the go-ahead to do his best solo during a musical piece called "Diminuendo and Crescendo in Blue."

Saxophonist
Paul Gonsalves

Paul Gonsalves not only did his best, but played one of the greatest saxophone solos in the history of jazz! Duke's plan worked. People in the audience went wild. They started dancing in the aisles and standing on their chairs to cheer. They loved what they were hearing. The next day, newspaper reporters wrote about what had happened.

After the Newport Jazz Festival, Duke and his orchestra were popular once again. For the rest of his life, Duke kept busy writing music and giving concerts all over the world.

Duke Ellington died in 1974. He was one of the first composers to show that jazz could be more than just popular dance music. He showed that jazz could be as beautiful and important as classical music.

Today it's as easy as ever to hear Duke Ellington's music on radio and television specials. Hundreds of his recordings can be found on compact discs and cassette tapes.